PEOPLE PA

Tudor Children

Haydn Middleton

Raintree

www.raintreepublishers.co.uk
Visit our website to find out
more information about
Raintree books.

To order:

☎ Phone 0845 6044371

📄 Fax +44 (0) 1865 312263

💻 Email myorders@raintreepublishers.co.uk

Customers from outside the UK please telephone +44 1865 312262

First published in Great Britain by Heinemann Library,
Halley Court, Jordan Hill, Oxford
OX2 8EJ, part of Harcourt Education.

Heinemann is a registered trademark of
Harcourt Education Ltd.

Editorial: Lucy Thunder and Helen Cox
Design: Jo Hinton-Malivoire, Richard Parker and
    Tinstar Design Limited (www.tinstar.co.uk)
Illustrations: Tokay Interactive Ltd
Picture Research: Rebecca Sodergren
Production: Séverine Ribierre

Originated by Ambassador Litho Ltd
Printed and bound in China
    by WKT Co. Ltd.

ISBN 978 0 431 14616 4 (hardback)
07 06 05 04 03
10 9 8 7 6 5 4 3 2 1

ISBN 978 0 431 14626 3 (paperback)
10
10 9 8 7 6 5 4

British Library Cataloguing in Publication Data
Middleton, Haydn
    Tudor Children. – (People in the past)
    305.2'3'0942'09031
A full catalogue record for this book is available   from
the British Library.

Acknowledgements
The publishers would like to thank the following for
permission to reproduce photographs:

AKG p16; Art Archive/Victoria and Albert Museum/Sally
Chappell p**6**; ATP p25; Bridgeman Art Archive/Christies
p23b; Bridgeman Art Library pp19, 26, 28, 32, 37;
English Heritage/National Monuments Record p30;
Fotomas Index pp29, 31; Hulton Getty pp9, 24; Mary
Evans Picture Library pp7, 15, 21; Museum of London
pp13, 36; National Portrait Gallery, pp33, 38; National
Trust Photographic Library pp23a (John Hammond),
34–5 (W H Rendell); Reproduction by kind permission
of Viscount De L'Isle, from his private collection at
Penshurst Place p41; Robert Erbe p27; The Royal
Collection 2000/Her Royal Majesty Queen Elizabeth II
pp10, 14; Tate Picture Library p12; Shakespeare Centre
Library p43; Woodmansterne Ltd p17.

Cover photograph of three Tudor children reproduced
with permission of Bridgeman Art Library.

The publishers would like to thank Rebecca Vickers for
her assistance with the preparation of this book.

Every effort has been made to contact copyright
holders of any material reproduced in this book. Any
omissions will be rectified in subsequent printings if
notice is given to the publishers.

Disclaimer
All the Internet addresses (URLs) given in this book
were valid at the time of going to press. However, due
to the dynamic nature of the Internet, some addresses
may have changed, or sites may have changed or
ceased to exist since publication. While the author and
Publisher regret any inconvenience this may cause
readers, no responsibility for any such changes can be
accepted by either the author or the Publisher.

Contents

Words appearing in the text in bold, **like this**, are explained in the Glossary.

The Tudor world

Five hundred years ago the world was a very different place. Europeans were only just realizing that America existed, and they had no idea about Australia. Meanwhile, the mighty **Ottoman Turks** were threatening to conquer the whole of Europe itself. And England (including the Principality of Wales) and Scotland were separate kingdoms, each with its own royal family.

From 1485 to 1603 the Tudor family ruled over England. We now call that period 'Tudor times'. The men, women and children who lived then we call 'Tudor people'. Some of these people were very rich. Many more were extremely poor. In this book you can find out what life was like for the children of both sorts of people.

There were only five Tudor **monarchs**, and the last three were all children of Henry VIII. Henry himself was the son of the first Tudor, Henry VII.

A world unlike ours

The everyday world of Tudor people – rich and poor alike – was not much like ours. About half the number of children born died before their first birthday. Yet the number of people kept rising fast. Maybe half the population was under 20 years of age.

The majority of Tudor people lived in country villages, not in cities, although there *were* big cities, like London, Bristol and Norwich, in Tudor times.

The Tudor family

The Tudor family ruled England and Wales from 1485 until 1603:
King Henry VII (king from 1485 to 1509)
King Henry VIII (king from 1509 to 1547)
King Edward VI (king from 1547 to 1553)
Queen Mary I (queen from 1553 to 1558)
Queen Elizabeth I (queen from 1558 to 1603)

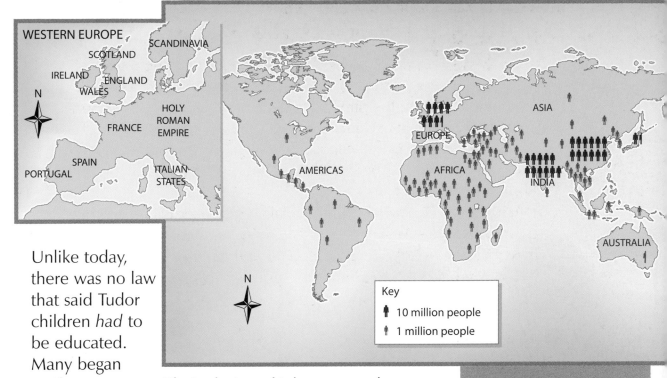

Unlike today, there was no law that said Tudor children *had* to be educated. Many began work very young. Their choice of jobs was much more limited than it is now. Most boys followed in their fathers' footsteps and did farm work of some kind. Girls were expected simply to marry, then look after their own families and maybe make cloth in their homes.

As you will find in this book, we know more about the rich than the poor, since more records about them have survived. But we can still use lots of clues to find out how poor children lived.

This map gives a rough idea of the size of the world's **population** in early Tudor times. There were far more people living in Europe and Asia than in the rest of the world, and hardly any in America. Europe was split into different countries, some of which are shown here.

Tudor money note

In this book, Tudor sums of money are shown in pounds (£), shillings (s) and pennies (d). There were 12d in a shilling, and 20s in a pound – which was worth a lot more then! Most people earned less than £10 in a whole year, and you could go to the theatre for a single penny.

The Tudor household

What is a typical British family like today? That is hard to answer. It all depends on how rich or poor the family is, where it lives, how many people are in it, and so on. It is just as hard to say what a typical Tudor family was like. Tudor families came in all shapes and sizes. Some lived in palaces. Others were so poor, they had to sleep under hedges.

In certain Tudor homes, not all the people were related to one another. Some of them were servants. Other non-relatives could be young **apprentices** or just children 'on loan' from other families (see pages 18 to 19). The family plus everyone else made up what was called the 'household'.

Domestic discipline

The person in charge of the entire household was the head of the family. Almost always, this was a man. He had great power. 'He is the highest in the family …,' wrote William Gouge in his book *Domesticall Duties*. 'He is like a king in his own home.'

The family of a wealthy Tudor man, Thomas More. Richer families tended to be bigger than poorer ones, partly because the rich could afford to have more children. In their spacious homes, they were also more likely to have more distant relatives living with them.

'The family that prays together, stays together,' is an old saying. This Tudor father is explaining a religious point to his family.

Tudor fathers – helped by their wives – expected to be obeyed by the children around them. Tudor books on child-rearing made it clear that 'a youth is just an untamed beast'. The most popular book of all, the Bible, also said: 'If you **smite** him with the rod, you shall deliver his soul from Hell.'

As England changed from a **Catholic** into a **Protestant** country, many parents took such words more seriously than before, and sometimes inflicted severe beatings on children. So did some Tudor teachers. They believed it was their duty to drive 'sinfulness' out of the young. Then, by learning obedience and discipline, children would grow into good, God-fearing adults.

Household sizes

In 1599 a **census** was taken at Ealing, near London. There were 404 people living in 85 households. This meant that four to five people probably lived in each one. In richer households there tended to be more people, including servants and more distant relatives. Some members of these families were grandparents – but only a minority of men and women lived that long. Like today, most families consisted of just two generations under one roof: parents and children. These are called 'nuclear' families.

Hazards of childbirth

On 13 October 1564, a newborn baby was christened in the **parish** church of Morebath, a tiny Devon village. We can read his name – Christopher Goodman – in the parish register of **baptisms**, deaths and marriages. We also read that another child was born that day – Christopher's twin. This child did not survive. The **midwife christened** it 'Creature'.

Maybe she gave it this odd name after only its head appeared. So she might not yet have known if it was a boy or a girl. But she had no time to wait. People believed that christening saved a dying child's soul from hell. It also meant that 'Creature' could then be given a Christian burial in a churchyard. Eight days later there was another funeral at Morebath – that of the mother of baby Christopher and 'Creature'.

A brood of children

Such sad stories were quite common in Tudor times. Childbirth could be highly dangerous for baby and mother alike. There were no hospital births, no antiseptics for operations, and very little medicine to ease the pain.

It was seen as a wife's role to have a brood of children and so most mothers had more children than today. After marrying in their mid-twenties, they could look forward to about fifteen years of having children and rearing them.

Napier's casebook

Richard Napier was a doctor and **astrologer**. In his casebook he recorded details about the patients he treated. These included John Flesher, whose wife died in childbirth, and then the baby died, too. As a result, wrote Napier, Flesher was 'very sorrowful and apt to weep; and at other times very angry.' He also described the misery of many mothers whose children had died. After Ellen Craftes' child was crushed by a door 'her head, heart and stomach became ill, her eyes dimmed with grief that she cannot see well.'

Poorer mothers breast-fed their babies. Whilst breast-feeding, they were unlikely to become pregnant again. So in poorer families there could be gaps of two years or more between births. A mother might then have five to seven children in all. Many of these died at birth or in childhood. Some parents in early Tudor times gave more than one of their children the same name. They did not seem to worry that this might cause confusion. The modern historian Lawrence Stone wrote that perhaps they accepted that one would die before growing up. The Timewell family, which also lived in Morebath, had three sons – all named John!

A German picture from 1513 showing a woman about to give birth. The person kneeling in front of her is a midwife. Births took place at home, not in hospitals.

A son and heir

People today are free to decide who gets their property after they die. They write legal documents called 'wills', to make clear who should receive what. A parent might divide everything up equally between his or her children. Or they might leave all their goods and money to someone else entirely. Many Tudor people made wills too, but in wealthy families almost all the property went to the eldest son. This system was called 'primogeniture' – from the Latin words meaning 'first-born'.

King Henry VIII is shown here with his third wife, Jane Seymour – mother of his only surviving, **legitimate** son, Prince Edward.

Rich Tudor parents were therefore keen to have a boy baby as soon as possible. He would be the male 'heir' to the family fortune. (And unlike a daughter, he would carry on the family name, since a Tudor woman had to take her husband's name when she married.) Ideally, rich parents wanted *two* sons. Then if the first died during childhood, his brother could become the new heir. In this way, there would be 'an heir and a spare'!

Family tensions

There was another reason why some Tudor parents preferred boy babies to girls. Girls could turn out to be much more expensive. When a daughter got married, her parents had to give some money to the father of the man she was to marry (the groom). This sum was called a 'marriage portion' or a 'dowry'. In return, the groom's family agreed to support the girl if the groom died before she did.

So money did not buy happiness for all the children in rich families. Younger sons often had to make their own way in the world; they might become soldiers or merchants or make a career in the church. Daughters depended on making 'a good marriage'. Often the younger brothers envied the eldest son, who was going to inherit so much.

Things were less complicated in poorer families. Although they had less property, many parents made sure in their wills that *all* their children received a share.

Only men can rule?

A king passed on to his eldest son not just his property but the crown as well. (Until Tudor times, people generally thought that a woman could not possibly rule the country.) King Henry VIII was so desperate to have a healthy male 'heir and a spare' that he got married six times. Only one of his wives, Jane Seymour, gave birth to a son who survived, Edward. He was crowned king after his father in 1547, but died six years later with no son of his own to take over. Then England had not just one woman ruler, but two: first Edward's half-sister Mary, who soon died, too, then his half-sister Elizabeth. She was an extremely successful and powerful queen, ruling for almost half a century.

Bringing up baby

There were no such things as Tudor baby-gro outfits. In fact, babies were wrapped up so tight, it was as if their parents wanted to *stop* them from growing! For the first months after birth, they were bound in cloth bandages that made it impossible for them to move the head or arms. After four months or so, their arms were freed, but not yet their legs.

Swaddling

Infants were wrapped up, or 'swaddled' like this for medical reasons. Tudor people believed that 'the tender limbs of a child may easily and soon bow and bend and take various shapes.' The tight cloths were meant to help them to grow straight. Many people also feared that unless babies were swaddled, they might do terrible damage to themselves – like ripping off their own ears! Wrapping up babies suited Tudor parents, too. Modern experiments have shown that swaddling slows down a baby's heartbeat, makes it sleep longer and cry less. Tudor parents also kept their babies out of harm's way by hanging the swaddled bundles up on wall pegs!

These wealthy sisters from the Cholmondeley family hold their first-born babies in a picture from around 1600. It is unlikely that either the women or their children wore such fine clothes when not posing for a painting!

This early Tudor rocking cradle had solid sides, which protected the baby from draughts.

Mother or nurse?

Modern mothers can choose whether to breast-feed their new babies or give them formula milk (a substitute for milk made from powder) in bottles. Some Tudor mothers had a different choice – whether to feed their infants themselves, or hire a **wet nurse** to feed them. Upper-class mothers might send their babies away for up to eighteen months to be fed and looked after in this way.

The children of richer Tudor families had to get used to seeing little of their parents. After being wet-nursed, many were brought up mainly by nurses, governesses and tutors, and some might then be sent to boarding school at age ten.

Sad results of wet-nursing

Wet-nursing was not always a happy experience for children. In a book called *Civil Conversation* (1581), the writer Stephen Guazzo tells the story of a child that says to its mother: 'You carried me for only nine months in your belly, but my wet nurse kept me with her for two years … As soon as I was born, we were separated, so I never got to know you.' The historian Lawrence Stone also points out that wet-nursed babies seemed twice as likely to die as babies fed by their own mothers.

Children without parents

Not all Tudor children were lucky enough to have two parents alive. Maybe 20 per cent of children under ten suffered the death of a mother or father and many became orphans.

If a child's parent married again, the child would get a stepmother or stepfather. But it seems that few children actually lived with their step-parents. Instead they went off to live with grandparents or uncles and aunts. If they had no relatives to support them, local officials had to make sure they were cared for, at places like Christ's Hospital in London. Some Tudor children had only mothers, even though their fathers were still alive. Divorces were not allowed by the Church, but parents did split up. In the city of Norwich in 1570, 8.5 per cent of the poor women in a survey had been deserted by their husbands.

Elizabeth I as a young princess. Her father Henry VIII grew tired of her mother, Anne Boleyn, and had her executed in 1536. Their marriage was declared 'null and void', which meant that Elizabeth became officially illegitimate. But she still became queen in 1558.

Henry Fitzroy, the illegitimate son of King Henry VIII by his lover Elizabeth Blount. He died aged seventeen. Some said he was poisoned by Henry's queen at the time, Anne Boleyn.

Punishing unmarried parents

Then there were **illegitimate** children. Their parents never got married at all. In Tudor times, if a child was born without married parents, it was seen as a bad thing. Such a child was called 'baseborn', meaning that its parents were sinners, so it was sinful, too. In Terling, Essex, between 1570 and 1640, 71 illegitimate births were recorded. In 61 of these cases, the parents were made to appear in court. If convicted, they were whipped and put in the **stocks**. Even if the mother had expected to marry the father and was abandoned, she was still punished.

Why were local officials so harsh about this? Partly they were concerned about expense. If an illegitimate child was poor, then the other families of the **parish** had to look after it. Partly too they feared that God would be displeased, and 'pour down His **wrath**' on the whole community.

Help from godparents

It was usual for Tudor boys to have two godfathers and a godmother. Tudor girls had a godfather and two godmothers. Such people might help out if their godchildren became orphans. We know from wills that people often left them money or goods. A Devonshire **yeoman** William Honeywell left £6 to his godson in his will, while in 1602, during a dinner visit to his god-daughter, he gave her a shilling. And in a letter of 1611, Lady Elizabeth Grey sent 'my most dearest love to my sweetest god-daughter' – showing that such relationships could be affectionate, too.

Staying alive

Alice George was an ordinary Oxford woman, born in 1572. She told a clergyman, John Locke, that 'she was married at thirty, and had fifteen children; that is, ten sons and five daughters **baptized**, besides three **miscarriages.**' Many of these children died before growing up. In the Devon village of Colyton, nearly a third of all children born between 1550 and 1750 died before they were fifteen years old. And in crowded, germ-ridden towns and cities, it was even harder to stay alive. During the reign of Elizabeth I, a person could expect to live on average for just 37 years.

Poor hygiene, widespread disease

Disease was a constant fact of life for Tudor children. Poor children, especially town-dwellers, were the most at risk. Living in cramped, unhygienic conditions, and suffering from bad diets, they often fell ill. Doctors were few and expensive. Even they did not really know how to diagnose or treat most diseases. Disastrous **epidemics** swept whole regions. Attacks of influenza (flu) in 1557 and 1558 killed about five per cent of the population. Those who died had already been weakened by hunger after serious harvest failures in 1555 and 1556.

These Tudor tombs can be found in Westminster Abbey, London. Only wealthy parents could afford to mark their children's deaths in this way.

A chilling picture of 'a child taken by Death' from its home and family. The relatives' reactions show that even though death was common, it still caused great misery.

Sanitation in most homes was poor or non-existent. Men and women seldom washed, and children seem not to have been toilet trained by adults. (But evidence survives of bed-wetters being made to drink a pint of their own urine – as a 'lesson'!)

Many parents, however, behaved fondly towards growing children. The modern historian Lawrence Stone writes that they tended 'to treat children from about two to seven as amusing pets' for the entertainment of grown-ups. 'It was,' he goes on, 'the one period in a child's life when his parents and other adults treated him other than harshly or with **indifference**.'

Skulls and earthworms

Only children from wealthy families could afford to be treated by doctors. Yet some Tudor doctors' cures had little to do with medical science. For **gout**, live earthworms were put on the affected skin until they began to smell. Other medicines might include powdered human skull. Many people worked out their own theories about illnesses and cures. If a root, leaf, nut or plant *looked* like a part of the human body, then it might bring health to that part. So walnuts, for example, were supposed to be good for the brain and for mental disease.

Home from home

Sir Simonds D'Ewes was born to upper-class parents in late Tudor times. As a man he wrote an **autobiography**, describing his childhood. Other boys from wealthy families may have had similar experiences. After several months with a **wet nurse**, he went to live with his grandparents for seven years. His parents visited him only twice, and he was brought up mainly by servants. He was sent to five different boarding schools. Then finally, aged sixteen, he went to St John's College, Cambridge, to be a student. He had spent almost all his young life away from home.

'Fostering out'

Tudor children of all classes had to get used to living in other people's houses. In early Tudor times, noble and other well-to-do parents often sent their children to live in households similar to their own. There they would learn how to behave at court. But in later Tudor times, boys like Simonds D'Ewes more usually went to private boarding schools, which only the rich could afford.

Rich farmers and merchants might also send their sons away – and even some daughters – to be **apprentices**. This would happen between the ages of seven and seventeen. Apprentices would live in their masters' houses, even if these houses were not very far away.

Absent fathers

In some wealthy Tudor families, the fathers – not the children – were 'exported' to homes elsewhere. **Courtiers** spent more time with their **monarchs** than with their children. Another man who chose to live apart from his family for long periods was the playwright William Shakespeare. Born in 1564 and brought up in Stratford-upon-Avon, Shakespeare lived and worked mainly in London through the 1590s. So his three children – who stayed in Stratford with their mother – saw little of their famous father. Sadly the only boy, Hamnet, died in 1596, at the age of just eleven.

Craftspeople and **artisans** usually apprenticed their sons to others, rather than give them work at home. And the children of labourers might be sent away to be farm servants or **domestic** servants in their early teens.

Only English parents seem to have 'fostered out' or 'exported' their growing children in this way. They began to do it in **medieval** times, but historians are still not quite sure why. It must have had a big effect on relationships between the generations.

Lady Tasburgh of Norfolk, pictured with her children. Married Tudor noblewomen, unlike their husbands, were not expected to spend time at court. Their children grew up in the country, seeing little of their father.

Skills for life

Hugh Latimer was the son of a **yeoman**. He went on to become the Bishop of Worcester. He remembered that his father taught him how to use a bow and arrow as a boy. 'As I got older and stronger,' he wrote, 'he brought me bigger and bigger bows.' People believed you could become a good archer only if you learned what to do while you were growing up.

In earlier Tudor times, it was vital that boys *did* learn this skill. Since 1285, all men from sixteen to 60 had a duty to fight for their **monarch** in times of emergency. The kind of weapons they used varied depending on how rich or poor the fighter was. For most, it was bows and arrows. Under Queen Elizabeth I, weapons like **pikes** and **harquebuses** became more common – and special training was given to young men who showed skill in using them.

Preparing for court

On pages 28 to 33, you can find out what schooling Tudor boys and girls were given. But either in or out of school, they were also meant to pick up other useful skills for life. For wealthy Tudors this included training for court.

Dancing was learned in the early years, not just for enjoyment but also – in the words of Lord Herbert of Cherbury – 'since it encourages suppleness and agility in the limbs.'

Swimming

There were no swimming pools in Tudor England. But children who lived near rivers or the sea still had the chance to swim. 'It is fit for a gentleman to learn how to swim, unless he gets cramps easily. However, I must confess that I myself cannot swim. For since I once nearly drowned while learning to swim, my mother forbade me to continue …'
From the **autobiography** of Lord Herbert of Cherbury (1583–1648).

According to Roger Ascham, who tutored Queen Elizabeth as a girl, 'to ride, **joust**, use all weapons, run, leap, dance, sing and play all instruments tunefully, **hawk**, hunt and play tennis are all necessary for a **courtier**. He should also learn several languages.'

This preparation was only for boys though. Wealthy young ladies were expected to learn music, singing, dancing and needlework. With these, they could expect to attract a suitable husband. Poorer girls had to learn as soon as possible how to cook, clean and run a household. This prepared them for when they married and set up homes of their own.

Peasant girls were trained in domestic duties from an early age. These women are washing cloth, beating it out, then hanging it up to dry or laying it out to bleach in the sun.

Children or adults?

When do children start being adults? When they get a full-time job? When they leave home? When they start to vote? When they get their driving licences? Different people would give different answers. But most people now would agree that there *is* a period of time called 'childhood'. And during that period, children have their own kinds of clothing, interests and activities. In Tudor times, it was not quite like that.

Growing up fast

Even small Tudor children were trained to behave like miniature adults. They looked like miniature adults, too. Little rich girls were stuffed into **bodices** and **corsets** reinforced with iron and whalebone. These were meant to shape their bodies in a way that the Tudors found attractive. Yet they could also cripple growing girls, breaking ribs and preventing the lungs from developing.

Boys might wear smocks (overalls, like shirts) until they were 'breeched'. This was when they got their first pair of knee-length trousers or 'breeches'. After this important moment, around the age of six, they were expected to be men in all but name.

Showing respect

Tudor children were rarely allowed to be 'childish', yet they had to show great respect to their parents. When at home, they had to kneel and ask for their parents' blessing every morning. They still had to do this when they visited as adults. Even grown-up sons had to keep their hats off in their parents' presence. Later in the 1600s an Oxford University student began his letters home with 'Most honoured father.' His father's replies began with the single word, 'Child'!

Wealthy Tudor children in clothing that made them look like 'miniature adults'. The girl was only 23 months old. The boy in knee-length trousers had been 'breeched' around the age of six.

Confirmation

The next key stage in growing-up came when children were **confirmed** in church. This happened between the ages of fourteen and sixteen. By sixteen, boys could also be 'called up' to fight for their **monarch**. Many of these boys – and their sisters – had already been doing adult work for five years or more.

It is hard to say exactly what a 'Tudor childhood' was. Most Tudor children had little time to themselves – and little space, too, since only the rich had separate rooms for each family member. Unlike today, very few products were made for just children to enjoy – even toys were far more rare. In Tudor times you were expected to grow up fast – then stay grown-up.

Children in need

'In the **parish** of St Stephen's there lives John Burr, 54 years old, who is too sick to work any more. His wife Alice, 40, spins. They have seven children, aged 20, 12, 10, 8, 6, 4 and 2. They can all spin wool, and have always lived in his house.'

That comes from a **census** of the poor in the city of Norwich in 1570. Many town and city families were terribly poor. In earlier Tudor times local officials often made door-to-door collections to help them out. Wealthier people were also generous in giving to the poor. But the problem was so great that from 1563, Tudor governments *made* the more fortunate support the poor of the parish. By law, people now had to pay a regular 'rate' or amount. This rate varied, according to how well-off they were themselves.

Children on the roads

Some poor families moved around the country – begging, looking for work, sometimes stealing. Tudor officials treated such people more harshly – returning them to their home parishes by force, among other punishments. By a law of 1547, **vagrant** children could be seized by anyone prepared to teach them a trade.

A Tudor family takes to the roads. As the population rapidly grew, there were not always enough jobs to go round. Some fathers took their wives and children with them on a search for work. But they could be confused with wandering criminals and beggars, and punished severely.

Beware vagrants!

In 1566 the writer Thomas Harman published a **pamphlet** warning people about the tricks that Tudor rogues and pickpockets got up to. Some vagrant children, he wrote, looked ill or wounded. But he said their beggar-parents might well have injured them on purpose – so that people would give them money out of pity. Vagrant babies were tied in sheets and carried on their mothers' backs. 'They bring the children up savagely,' wrote Harman.

Boys might then be **apprenticed** until they were 24, girls until they were 20. The children's parents had no say in this at all. If a child ran away and was recaptured, he or she could be treated as a slave.

Orphaned children had difficulties, too, if they could not prove where their home parish was. Local officials were unsure where a poor girl named Catherine Boland had been born. She spent some time in Northamptonshire and some in the city of Leicester. But both **parishes** refused to take responsibility for her, and shuffled her back and forth. In the end, government officials called **Justices of the Peace** ordered both parishes to share the cost of her upkeep.

Wealthy townspeople, like Humphrey and Elizabeth Bridges in Cirencester, gave very generously to the poor. The words on their tomb in the parish church mention how generous they were.

Working children

Many people today go to university after school. They do not usually start regular jobs until they are over twenty. In Tudor times almost all children began to work at a much younger age.

In 1563 a law called the Statute of **Artificers** was passed. The law said that any poor, unemployed male from 12 to 60 years of age could be *made* to work in farming. Boys and men could, for example, be forced to work in the fields during the hay or corn harvests.

Training for the future

The law of 1563 also set new rules on **apprenticeship**. Unless a young man had been trained by a master for seven years, he was not allowed to be employed in any specialist trade or craft. If a boy wanted to become a **draper**, a goldsmith or a merchant – all of them 'superior' jobs – he could do so only if his father did the job already, or if his family was quite wealthy.

All over Europe, girls and boys helped to gather in the autumn hay before rain could spoil it. Hay was used as food for animals over the long winter months. Farm-workers' young children also did jobs like chasing away birds, watching sheep, milking cows and making butter and cheese.

This is an 'indenture' – a written agreement between a master and an apprentice, setting out what will happen during the apprenticeship.

Boys could be as young as seven when they agreed to train with a master. Sometimes their apprenticeships lasted for up to ten years. For most of this time, they were not paid for their work. So, by the end, they could be doing a man's work for no wages.

Why was the government so keen on this lengthy training? Partly it wanted to ensure that adult butchers, bakers, clockmakers or shipbuilders worked only to the highest standards. Partly, too, it did not want too many boys training for a limited number of jobs.

Apprentices were not just taught by their masters. They were housed, fed and clothed by them, too. Some masters treated their apprentices well, and gave them a good education. In the 1580s, 82 per cent of boy apprentices in London and Middlesex could read and write. Other masters were so harsh that the boys ran away.

Small children, big earners

'In English cities every child of six or seven years old is forced to some art in which he earns his own living and something else to enrich his parents or master. In the city of Norwich, children aged six to ten make fine knitted stockings. Every child over 7 is able to earn 4 shillings a week at that trade.' The Tudor writer Thomas Wilson made these remarks in *The State of England in 1600*. It is highly unlikely that these child workers were allowed to keep much of the money they earned for themselves.

Schools for all?

According to the Tudor schoolmaster and writer Richard Mulcaster, education was meant to train every person 'to perform those functions in life which his position shall require.' Most men needed no book-learning to work at their jobs in the fields, so, as boys they got little or no schooling. And since most adult women were expected to concentrate on 'good **housewifery**', girls were not usually educated either. But as you will see over the next six pages, there were several changes in Tudor education – and more children than before benefited from them.

Religious-based education

In the Middle Ages almost all England's schools were run by the Church. 'Song' and 'grammar' schools were attached to cathedrals or abbeys. Boys went to them to train to sing in church services or train to be priests. During the 1500s, local rich men paid to start up schools that were less religious. But teachers still had to get a licence to teach from their local bishop. And any teacher who tried to 'keep a school' without a licence could be **excommunicated** – a very serious punishment.

A child learning the alphabet. Schools did not always have highly-qualified staff. In Falmouth, in Cornwall, poor Tudor children got a basic education from the local bellringer.

Younger children used a 'hornbook', like this. Inside the wooden frame was a single page, protected by a thin clear sheet of horn.

By the end of Tudor times, young boys (aged five or six in towns, seven or eight in the country) might go to 'petty' schools for a short time. There they learned first reading, then writing. Some girls might go to these schools, too. But by 1600, 72 per cent of men and 92 per cent of women could still not sign their own names.

At 'grammar schools', older boys learned Latin and maybe some Greek until they were fifteen. Poor children were allowed to go to these schools for free, but often parents needed them to work to bring in extra money. Meanwhile, wealthy parents paid fees for their sons to be boarders at new private secondary schools.

University education

There were just two universities in Tudor England, at Oxford and at Cambridge. In early Tudor times, boys went to the colleges there when aged fourteen or fifteen. By 1600, new students tended to be older and there were about 2000 students in all at each university. William Harrison wrote in 1577 that the colleges were built 'at first only for poor men's sons, whose parents were not able to bring them up to learning. But now … the rich take many of the places.' Some gentleman students then completed their education by studying law at the 'Inns of Court' in London.

At grammar school

In his play *As You Like It*, William Shakespeare described:
'… the whining schoolboy, with his satchel
And shining morning face, creeping like snail
Unwillingly to school.'
Was he writing from personal experience? If so, from the age of
about six he probably went to the King's New School in his home
town of Stratford-upon-Avon. In southern England, many new
grammar schools like it began to appear after 1550. Between
1558 and 1603, 136 were founded. More of the masters were
well-trained at university, too. Boys like the young Shakespeare
(from families of **yeomen**, craftspeople, merchants or tradespeople)
were now able to get a good education.

The gateway to all knowledge

Teaching varied from school to school, but most schoolwork
was based on the study of Latin – the gateway to 'all knowledge
whatsoever'. Across western Europe Latin was still written and
spoken by clergymen, scholars, politicians, officials, lawyers and
doctors. Schoolboys read and translated comedies by Ancient
Roman playwrights, as well as the work of great poets like Ovid.
There were few books, so long passages were learned by heart.

This photo shows
the schoolroom
at the Grammar
School, Stratford-
upon-Avon, set up
much as it would
have looked in
Tudor times. The
pupils had to attend
lessons up to ten
hours a day, six days
a week. No wonder
school holidays
were sometimes
called 'remedies'!

Tudor pupils used small, cheap books like this to learn simple Latin phrases. During Tudor times, English began to take the place of Latin as the language used for education.

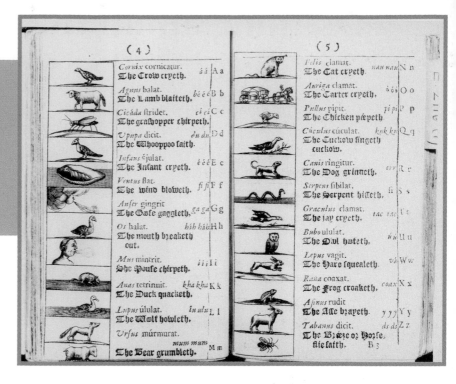

Some of the classwork was acted out in short plays. There might also be a little Greek, if the masters were qualified to teach it. But history, geography, arithmetic and English barely figured as separate subjects.

As in the home, discipline was usually strict. Some masters struck a naughty pupil's hand or mouth with a 'ferrula' – a flat piece of wood, pear-shaped at the end, with a hole in the middle. Others beat the pupil's naked bottom with a bundle of birch twigs. According to a popular Dutch author called Batty, God had *designed* the human buttocks to be severely beaten without causing serious injury to the victim!

Westminster School rules, 1560

Tudor schools were quite small compared to today's. At Westminster School there were only two masters. Their duties were: 'to teach and examine in Latin, Greek and Hebrew grammar, and the **humanities**, poets and **orators**. Also to see that the boys behave properly in church, school, hall and chamber, as well as in all walks and games, that their faces and hands are washed, their heads combed, their hair and nails cut, their clothes both linen and woollen, gowns, stockings and shoes kept clean, neat, and like a gentleman's … They shall choose **monitors** from among the most serious scholars to stop anything dirty being done.'

Learning at home

No law said Tudor parents *had* to send their children to school. Some wealthy families paid teachers to give lessons in the home. Henry VIII's chief minister Thomas Cromwell employed a full-time tutor to educate his son, Gregory. Around 1530, the tutor described a typical day they spent together. The pupil must have missed the company of other boys his own age:

After prayers, Gregory looked at a passage called 'Youthful **Piety**' by the great Dutch scholar Erasmus. He had to read it in Latin and in English, then compare the two. Then he practised writing for one or two hours, and spent the same amount of time reading a history of England by Robert Fabian. The rest of the day he spent playing the **lute** and **virginals**. 'When he goes riding,' his tutor added, 'I talk to him on the way about Roman or Greek history. Then I ask him to tell it back to me. To relax he goes hunting and **hawking** and shoots his long bow, very skilfully.'

A rare picture of an unusual sight in Tudor times: a female teacher with a female pupil. Some girls from wealthy families became great scholars.

This painting is thought to be of Lady Jane Grey (1537–1554). She was famous for her learning, writing to leading scholars in Europe by the time she was fourteen, and reading Greek for fun!

New learning for girls

'I do not see why girls should not learn as well as boys,' wrote the scholar and politician Sir Thomas More. Several other experts in education agreed with him. So, from about 1520 to 1560 tutors taught a number of upper-class English girls Latin, Greek, French and Italian to a very high level.

Later in the century, however, educational fashions changed again. Girls were now expected to return to learning 'social graces' like music, painting, drawing, dancing and needlework. They were also not meant to 'challenge' their menfolk in the home. Maybe educated women seemed threatening to men! Whatever the reason, the experiment in girls' education did not continue.

Top scholar

In his book *The Schoolmaster*, the tutor Roger Ascham (1515–1568) described one of his pupils – a girl – as 'one example for all the gentlemen of this [royal] court to follow.' 'One maid goes beyond you in excellence of learning and knowledge of many languages … Besides her perfect fluency in Latin, Italian, French and Spanish, she now reads more Greek every day than some priests read Latin in a whole week. And best of all, she has worked hard … to understand, speak and write more cleverly than almost anyone at the two universities.' Who was this amazing scholar? Henry VIII's daughter, later Queen Elizabeth I!

Special days

Tudor children did not have holidays like ours. But they had plenty of time off work or school to celebrate special days in the Church calendar. Most fell in the six months between 24 December and 24 June. Writer John Aubrey looked back and described the Tudor village festivals of his grandfather's time:

'In every **parish** there is, or was, a church house. Inside it were spits, crockery, all kinds of **utensils** for making a feast. Here the housekeepers met, and were merry and gave charity to the poor. The young people came there too, and had dancing, bowling, shooting at targets, etc, while the older folk sat watching … Such joy and merriment took place every holiday.'

Festival fun and games

The longest festival period was the twelve days of Christmas, from 25 December to 6 January. Then there would be decorations, singing, house visits, plays put on by mummers (silent actors) and games of football. More Church festivals and saints' days followed – like Plough Monday, Shrove Tuesday, St Valentine's Day and Easter – until the high excitement of May Day. At that time young and old people alike would spend the night celebrating out of doors, then bring home a maypole to dance around.

Boy Bishops

In some cathedrals, abbeys and university colleges at Christmas, a boy was chosen to dress up as a bishop and take some church services for fun. At Salisbury Cathedral the choirboys chose one of their own number to be the 'Boy Bishop'. At King's College, Cambridge, he wore a small costume including a white wool coat, a scarlet gown with a white fur hood, fine knitted gloves, gold rings, with a **crozier** and a **mitre**. Even some local parishes had Boy Bishops. They led processions through the streets, collecting money that was then handed over to the church.

Not everyone was so keen on the fun. 'There is a great Lord among them all,' wrote John Stubbes, a pamphlet (small booklet) writer from the 1580s, 'namely Satan, prince of hell.'

Stubbes obviously disapproved of such 'pastimes and sports'. So did other strict Christians like him, known as Puritans. But old customs were not easy to get rid of. And some were not just an excuse for merry-making. On Midsummer Eve, for example, people lit bonfires made of bones (this is where we get the word bonfires or 'bone-fires'). The stench was supposed to drive away various kinds of evil. This included both diseases that infected humans and wet weather or **blight** that ruined crops.

Even when no special festival was being celebrated, Tudor villagers could still let off steam. Husbands who let their wives 'henpeck' them – like the one being carried here – were paraded around the area. As they were taken on this 'skimmington ride', people played rough music and mocked them.

Having fun

Older relatives have probably said to you, 'When we were young, we had to make our own entertainment.' For poorer Tudor children with time to spare, that was certainly true.

Only wealthy parents could afford to buy carved and painted wooden toys – the most expensive dolls and toy ships often came from abroad. Nor did poor children get the chance to go riding, **hawking**, hunting or shooting like the better-off. But in the countryside they had more opportunity than most modern children to roam around and to swim or fish in local rivers and lakes.

Great shows

There were, of course, no televisions, cinemas, pop festivals or massive sporting events. But the Tudor **monarchs** laid on lavish **pageants** and processions to impress their subjects, sometimes by torchlight. In 1539 Henry VIII staged a mock-battle on large flat boats called barges on the River Thames in London. Actors playing 'the King's men' defeated those playing 'the **Catholic Pope's** men' and threw them all overboard. (This was just after Henry VIII had stopped England being a Catholic country.)

This wooden rocking horse has survived since Tudor times. It must have belonged to a wealthy family.

This 1560 painting from the Netherlands, called *Children's Games*, could almost be showing a playground scene in a modern school. But Tudor children somehow had to survive without mobile phones, personal stereos and replica football kits!

For more gruesome entertainment, children could join the crowds that watched public executions. And at festivals like Shrovetide (from the seventh Sunday before Easter until the end of the following Tuesday) some brutal street sports were played in the towns. One was football, which rarely had either teams or rules. According to Sir Thomas Elyot in 1531 it was 'nothing but beastly fury and extreme violence'. Another was 'cock-threshing' – in which a cockerel was tied up by one leg, while people threw missiles to knock it over or kill it. King Henry VII even had cockerels delivered to his palace at Shrovetide in 1493, so that he could watch them fight each other to the death!

Tudor drama

In earlier Tudor times, children could watch special Christian plays on Corpus Christi Day in June. These were called 'mystery plays'. They were put on by groups of tradespeople, and showed the history of the world from Adam and Eve to the present time. Children would have enjoyed the rude jokes and everyday language. The plays were last performed in England at Coventry in 1580. But children could still enjoy shows put on by bands of travelling actors. And some could afford to pay a penny and watch plays at the first purpose-built theatres – like The Globe on the South Bank of the River Thames in London.

Children on the throne

King Henry VIII tried hard to make sure his crown passed to a male heir. Only a king, he believed, could successfully rule England. Henry achieved his aim. When he died in 1547 he was succeeded by his son, who now became King Edward VI. Unfortunately Edward was just nine years old. 'Woe to thee, O land, where the king is a child,' said Bishop Hugh Latimer in a sermon in 1549. Why did he say this?

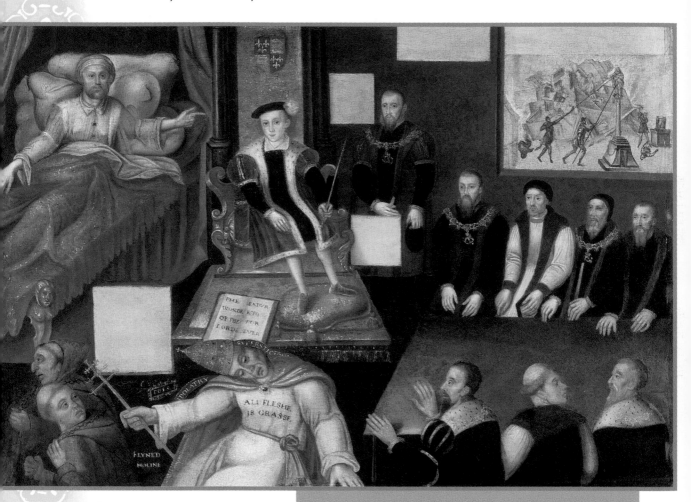

This painting from around 1568 shows Henry VIII on his deathbed in 1547. He points to the son who would become king after him – Edward VI. The man next to Edward is his uncle, the Duke of Somerset, who briefly ruled in his name.

The need for personal rule

Today a queen or king has little real power. But in Tudor times a ruler really had to rule. A mighty king like Henry VIII was able to strike fear and respect into his subjects (a bit like a headteacher!). They would then think twice before disobeying him. They also believed *God* would punish any disobedience, since all true kings had the blessing of Heaven. With a boy-king, things were different.

Edward VI was still a schoolboy. He was a good pupil in Latin, French and Greek, loved music and astronomy, and was deeply interested in religion. But his studies left him little time to rule. Besides, he was too young to inspire fear and respect. So his uncle the Duke of Somerset ran the kingdom for him. But some of Somerset's **policies** proved unpopular. People showed how unhappy they were by rebelling in several parts of England in 1549. They might not have rebelled against a real king. But they did rebel against the rule of Edward's 'evil **councillor**', Somerset.

Somerset was removed and the Duke of Northumberland took his place. But some now saw *him* as an 'evil councillor'. There could have been more rebellions, but in 1553 Edward died of **consumption**, aged only fifteen. No child would ever rule England again.

A child Queen of Scots

Mary Stuart was even younger than Edward VI when she became Queen of Scotland. When her father King James V died in 1542, she was just one week old. Talks began at once to arrange a marriage with the future King Edward of England. Royal children were often **betrothed** very early, to form a friendly link between their kingdoms. But in 1548 Mary sailed abroad instead to marry the future king of France. They married when she was sixteen. He died when she was only eighteen. Her sad story did not get any happier. She was executed for plotting against Edward VI's half-sister, Queen Elizabeth I of England, after spending nearly 20 years in prison.

Growing up into adults

Most Tudor parents strictly controlled their children. Many Tudor fathers decided what jobs their sons should do. Some also had a big say in whom their children would marry. In this way, children still felt their parents' influence long after they became adults.

Choosing whom to marry

Children from wealthy families tended to get married quite young. For this, they needed their parents' **consent**. Often the parents arranged 'good' marriages for them. Queen Elizabeth I's **Chancellor of the Exchequer**, Sir Walter Mildmay, chose a fourteen-year-old girl for his son Anthony to marry – against his son's own wishes!

Lord Burghley, Elizabeth I's chief minister, had this advice for his younger son: 'Take great care in the choice of your wife, for she may be the cause of all the good or ill that happens to you; and, as in warfare, you can make only one mistake … Find out about her character, and what her parents were like when they were young. Let her not be poor … yet do not choose someone ugly just because she is rich …'

Arranged marriages

In 1514 a Lancashire girl was forced by her **yeoman** relations to marry a man she deeply disliked. If she refused, they told her, she would lose her **inheritance** in land. But her new husband beat her badly, and she ran away from him, demanding a separation. 'I would not have stayed with him for an hour,' she explained, 'but I did not want to lose my land.' Another girl, Margery Shaftoe, found her future mapped out like this in her father's will of 1599: 'To my daughter Margery: 60 sheep, and I give her in marriage to Edward, son of Reynold Shaftoe of Thockerington.'

Staying single longer

Tudor people usually lived shorter lives than us, but most of them did not get married earlier. The average age for a bride was 26, for a groom it was around 28. By marrying quite late, people could limit the number of children they had.

Not all upper-class arranged marriages turned out to be loveless or unhappy. In 1584 Robert Sidney married Barbara Gamage. They had almost certainly never met before. But they enjoyed a happy life together until Robert died in 1626. This painting shows Lady Sidney with her children.

Many poorer children lived away from home. Without their parents watching over them, they were freer to choose their partners for life. But they still had to wait until they had finished their **apprenticeships**, and had enough money to set up a home. Then, when they could look after themselves and earn a living at last, they could start up families of their own.

How do we know? – Parish registers

In 1538 Thomas Cromwell, the chief minister of King Henry VIII, sent out royal 'injunctions' or orders to every **parish** priest. These injunctions ordered the priests to set up a parish register. In it they were to record information about the parish such as **christenings**, marriages and deaths. It provides a vital source of information about Tudor children for modern historians. This is what the injunctions said:

'You shall keep a register, in which you shall write the day and year of every wedding, christening and burying made within your parish. And every priest who comes after you must do likewise … For the safe keeping of this register, the parish shall supply one good **coffer** with two locks and keys ... Every Sunday you shall take this register out and … record all the weddings, christenings and burials made during the week before. Then the register must be locked up again. Failure to do this will result in a fine of 3s 4d, to go towards keeping the church in good repair.'

Valuable records

From about 1550 onwards, more and more parish registers survive. They were not always kept accurately, and historians have to be careful that the information they take from them is correct. But they can help us to see how life changed for children during the later Tudor period.

Single mothers in Morebath

The parish register of Morebath, a village in Devon, survives from 1558. In it, we can trace the arrival of every new child in the village. Not all these children, however, may have been very welcome. In March 1566 a son John was born to Margaret Morsse. And in November 1568 a son James was born to Mary Timewell. Neither Margaret nor Mary were married, for there is no record of their weddings in the register. Therefore their children were **illegitimate**. This was disapproved of by many Tudor people (see page 15).

We can tell, for example, that by 1600 the **birth rate** was rising. Partly this was because the average age of people getting married was falling. Partly it was because fewer children were being killed by the plague or a type of flu called 'the sweating sickness'.

A plague *did* strike Stratford-upon-Avon in the summer of 1564. The burial register shows that it probably killed more than 200 people. (From 1 January to 20 July, 22 burials were recorded. For the rest of the year there were 237.) One person who escaped the plague was a newly **baptized** baby – the future playwright, William Shakespeare. Like the parish registers, young William survived. Today we can also use *his* plays as a source of information on life in Tudor times.

This entry in the Stratford parish register tells us that William Shakespeare was christened on 26 April 1564. It says in Latin, 'William, son of John Shakespeare'. Babies were usually christened three days after they were born. But we cannot be sure of Shakespeare's exact birth date.

Timeline

1485	Tudor family begins to rule over England and Wales
1492	Christopher Columbus reaches America
1509–47	Reign of Henry VIII
1529–39	England stops being a Roman **Catholic** country
1536	King Henry VIII begins to close down the monasteries and nunneries, including some schools in these places
1538	**Parish** registers kept from now on
1542	Mary Queen of Scots is born
1547	Very harsh law passed against **vagrant** children
1547–53	Reign of boy-king Edward VI
1553–58	Reign of Mary I
1558–1603	Reign of Elizabeth I 136 new grammar schools set up
1563	First Tudor Poor Law passed, helping poorest families; Statute of **Artificers** passed, setting new rules on **apprenticeship** and work
1564–1616	Life of William Shakespeare
1577–80	Francis Drake becomes first English sea-captain to sail around the world
1580	Last 'mystery plays' in England performed at Coventry
1587	Mary Queen of Scots is executed by order of Elizabeth I
1588	English navy beats invading Spanish Armada (fleet of ships)
1603	End of Tudor period

Sources and further reading

Sources

The author and Publishers gratefully acknowledge the publications from which sources in the book are drawn. In some cases the wording or sentence structure has been simplified to make the material appropriate for a school readership.

Birth, Marriage and Death, David Cressy (Oxford, 1997)

Elizabeth I and Her Reign, Ed. Richard Salter (Macmillan Documents and Debates, 1988)

Elizabethan People, Ed. Joel Hurstfield and Alan G.R. Smith (Edward Arnold Documents of Modern History, 1972)

The Elizabethan Underworld, Gamini Salgado (Alan Sutton, 1984)

The Family, Sex and Marriage in England 1500–1800, Lawrence Stone (Pelican, 1979)

The Later Tudors, Penry Williams (Oxford, 1995)

Poverty and Vagrancy in Tudor England, John Pound (Longman, 1971)

The Sixteenth Century, Patrick Collinson (Oxford, 2002)

Tudor England, 1485–1603, Ed. Roger Lockyer and Dan O'Sullivan (Longman Sources and Opinions, 1993)

The Tudor Image, Maurice Howard (Tate Gallery, 1995)

The Voices of Morebath, Eamonn Duffy (Yale University Press, 2001)

Further reading

A Tudor School, Peter Chrisp (Heinemann Library, 1997)

Tudor World, Haydn Middleton (Heinemann Library, 2001)

Tudor Children, Jane Shuter (Heinemann Library, 1996)

Tudor Family Life, Jane Shuter (Heinemann Library, 1997)

Websites

www.heinemannexplore.co.uk – contains KS2 History modules including the Tudors.

www.brims.co.uk/tudors/ – information on Tudors for 7–10 year olds.

Glossary

apprentices young people learning a craft from a master

apprenticeship practice of learning a craft from a master

artificers craftsmen

artisans skilled men who work with their hands

astrologer someone who studies the heavens to make predictions

autobiography someone's life-story, written by him- or herself

baptism ceremony in which a child is made a member of the church

baptize make a child a member of the church

betrothed engaged to be married

birth-rate number of births per every 1000 people each year

blight plant disease caused by parasites

bodice part of a dress or undergarment above the waist

Catholic only Christian faith in western Europe until the 1520s, when people began to follow the new Protestant faith

census counting up of all the people in a country

Chancellor of the Exchequer person who deals with all money matters for a monarch or government

christen make a child a member of the church

confirmed going through the service of 'confirmation' in church, as long as you have been baptized before

consent agreement

consumption common Tudor disease affecting the lungs

coffer box for keeping valuable things in

corset tight-fitting undergarment

councillor adviser to the king or queen

courtier person who spent time at a king or queen's court as a companion or adviser

crozier long hooked staff carried by a bishop

domestic at home, in the home

draper seller of cloth

epidemics widespread diseases

excommunicated not allowed to worship in church any more; cut off from the Christian religion

gout disease affecting the joints and feet

harquebus early kind of gun that could be carried

hawking hunt birds or animals with a hawk

housewifery all the jobs done by a woman around the house

humanities study of non-scientific subjects

indifference lack of interest in someone or something

inheritance belongings and land received from another person

illegitimate child born to parents who are not married

joust competition to fight an opponent on horseback

Justices of the Peace local Tudor officials

legitimate born to married parents

lute guitar-like musical instrument

medieval during the Middle Ages (just before Tudor times)

midwife nurse who helps women give birth to their babies

miscarriage death of a baby before it is due to be born

mitre pointed hat of a bishop

monarch king or queen

monitor person who helps to keep order and organizes things

orator great public speaker

Ottoman Turks Turkish people who conquered large parts of eastern Europe and Asia

pageant procession for entertainment

parish local area with its own church and own church official

piety deep religiousness

pike Tudor weapon, like a spear

policies actions planned and carried out by a government

Pope head of the Catholic church. He lives in Rome.

population number of people in a country

Protestant religious faith of people who turned away from the teachings of the Catholic church

sanitation flushing toilets and drains

smite hit

stocks timber frame that criminals were locked up in, to be viewed in public by passers-by

utensils tools, objects used for a certain purpose

vagrant poor, wandering person

virginals Tudor musical instrument like a harpsichord

wet nurse woman who breast-feeds someone else's baby

wrath anger

yeoman rich farmer with his own land

Index